Money Is Simple

How The World Taught You Made It Complicated

Brian S. Stephens

Special Thanks to my Lord and Savior Jesus Christ
My Wife, Michele & Son Rayshawn, and Daughter Raven
My Family that raised me, and help shape my character;
Mom, Helen Stephens
Grandparents; Ernest and Lillie Mae Reese

———————

Our Finance Team; Maurice Goins, Pamela Greene,
Granville & Ilene White
James Saunders
Teresa Sanders
Danielle Sydnor - Thanks for teaching me about "Dream
Boards".
Asia Newell
Angela Wilcoxson
Sherri White

———————

Dr. John L. Dew Jr.
Liza Smith
Mendi Carrington
Breana Smith
Jason Carter
Freda Houchins
Nina Pettry
"Thank You" Amani Spicer who planted the first seed for
me writing this book

———————

Min. Harold Webb, Director of Christian Education
My Pastor; Kevin James for allowing me the chance to
teach the finance class
To New Community Bible Fellowship, thank you for
allowing me to play a small part in your life's journey

CONTENTS

- CHAPTER 1 -

HOW MUCH IS ENOUGH?

Let me start off by saying I am not a financial expert. I do not even work in the financial sector as a banker, broker or a financial analyst. I have just been blessed to teach a finance class for the past twelve years at my local church. I am just a regular man that always wondered how most people I've met never had enough money and always seemed to need more.

For example, a person who made $35,000 a year may think if they could just make $45,000, they would be okay. Then another person that made $45,000 may think their life would be better if they could just earn $55,000. Then one more person who made $55,000 a year may think if they could just get their hands on $65,000, things would work out. These scenarios could go on into the millions with the same, "I need more" mentality. Likewise, I have read articles and heard on television that there are people who make millions of dollars per year, but they are filing for bankruptcy and losing their homes to foreclosure. They, also, have creditors calling them and are having their cars repossessed.

As you can see, no matter the amount of annual income in those examples, they all concluded that they still needed a little more. I hope you noticed the pattern. All this made me ask the questions," What is the magic number?" "How much does it take to have a nice lifestyle?" That's why Chapter 1 of this book is titled, *"How much is enough?"*

Over time, I have found that there isn't any magical number, but there are two key things that are needed to make sure whatever you earn is enough: **Discipline** and **contentment.** Unfortunately, our society has gotten away from these two concepts of life. When **discipline** and **contentment** are practiced daily, the amount of money you need will align with your **purpose** and **vision**, which are two additional terms I will use throughout this book. After all, this book is simple, easy and practical enough for an average twelve-year old to understand, yet informative enough that college professors can glean some insight.

Now, before we get into the money side of things, let's talk briefly about **purpose** and **vision** using two similar scenarios. Let's say you are sixteen years old and just hanging out on a Friday night with your neighborhood friends at the basketball courts. The next thing you know, someone breaks out a pack of cigarettes and offers you one. At that moment, you say to yourself, I'm not really a smoker, but I'll do it this one time.

Plus, you don't have anything **planned** for Saturday, so you smoked due to peer pressure and wanting to fit in. Your **decision** was made as you only considered that present moment on that Friday night.

On the other hand, let's say you are sixteen years old and you are on the track team as a sprinter and a distance runner. It's Friday night and you have a Track meet Saturday morning. In this scenario, you are with some of your friends from the neighborhood and hanging out at the basketball courts and one of them lights up a cigarette and offers you one. You are not a smoker and are not influenced by the peer pressure that most sixteen-year olds experience. You have a **vision** of winning your events Saturday and that gives you the courage to say no to the cigarette and head home to rest up for the meet.

What are the differences in these two examples? The differences are in the **vision** and **purpose** that flashed across each individual's mind. In the first scenario, there were no **plans** beyond that Friday evening and peer pressure won the vote to smoke. In contrast, the second scenario showed that the **purpose** of the person resisting the offer to smoke had **visions** of winning all their events during that Saturday's track meet. It was the person in the second scenario that made a better decision because they knew their **purpose** and **vision** could have been hindered had they smoked.

Likewise, a forty-six-year-old woman received a $5,000 income tax return her sister, and best friend were encouraging her to go to Cancun for a week, to do some shopping and lay out on the warm, sunny beach because she deserves a get-a-way. In contrast, the woman knew the money would be better spent by putting $3,000 into her savings account and spending $2,000 on her car's transmission, which had been going bad for the last three months. Which one will she choose? It all depends on her **vision** and how determined she is to reach her **goals**. How much internal **discipline** does she have to withstand the peer pressure from her sister and best friend? Which one would you choose? You will be challenged to make choices and **decisions** your whole life and most **decisions** affect your money.

Having a **vision** and knowing your **purpose** helps you make better daily **decisions,** no matter what age you are. On the contrary, the opposite is true when you don't have a **vision** and you don't know your **purpose.** In these times, you will more than likely make poor **decisions** because you are just thinking short-term. The scripture found in Proverbs 29:18, part A, says it best, *"Where there is no **vision**, the people perish." KJV*

NOTES

- CHAPTER 2 -

SOME OF OUR SCHOOL SYSTEMS
LET US DOWN

When you were in Junior High or High School, you may have taken Pre-Algebra, Algebra, Geometry, Trigonometry or Calculus. I have nothing against advanced mathematics classes but, in most cases, unless you became some type of engineer or were fortunate enough to be part of the NASA Space program, you may not ever use that kind of math for your everyday life or your current job. Did your school teach you the Rule of 72? I'm sure most of you are wondering what it is. To my young readers, who may still be in school, this is not a reason to not learn or apply yourself to take the advance mathematic courses, but a good reason to ask your math teacher to teach you about it. The Rule of 72 is a simple math equation that tells you how long it will take for your money to double. For example, if you have $1,000 and it's earning 1% annual interest, it would take your $1,000 a total of 72 years (72 divided by 1% = 72 Years) to become $2,000.

Let's take the same $1,000, but it's earning 10% annual interest. So, this time you take 72 divided by 10%. Now your $1,000 will take seven years and two months to become $2,000. Do you see the importance of under-standing interest rates? It can be the difference between

72 years and seven years. I like to use whole numbers to make the math simple when dealing with interest rates.

However, the most important thing is that you understand the principles of the Rule of 72. To further demonstrate, let's say you have $10,000 that is earning annual interest at 1%. The math for this is 72 divided by 1% equals 72. So, in 72 years your $10,000 would become $20,000. Likewise, if that $10,000 was earning 10% interest annually, that would be 72 divided by 10%, which is 7.2. That means it would take seven years and two months for that $10,000 become $20,000. Do you see the trend? The amount of money doesn't matter, but the interest rate is critical.

The good news about the Rule of 72 in these examples is that they both were investments, which meant the money was earning interest. On the other hand, the sad news is the Rule of 72 still applies when you owe money that has an interest rate attached to it. In essence, the money is doubling as it goes away from you and this debt calculates differently, depending on the type of debt.

Typically, there are two basic types of debt: revolving and installment. Credit cards are a great example of revolving debt. This type of account has a different payment amount each month, depending on your current balance and interest rate.

Just like that revolving door on that big office building in your Downtown area that hundreds of people continue to use, so it is with your revolving debt on your credit card. You can use it as much as you like, as long as you don't exceed your credit limit. But remember, if you don't pay it off, in full, at the end of each month, then the Rule of 72 kicks in and you are paying interest on the money you borrowed.

To illustrate, let's say you have a $7,000 credit card balance with a 15% interest rate and your monthly payment is $150. It would take you five years and eleven months to pay off that $7,000 balance and you would have also paid $3,571 in interest. As a result, the total you would have paid is $10,571. Keep in mind, that's only if you didn't use that credit card anymore during that repayment period.

A car loan, on the other hand, is a familiar example of an installment debt. For instance, a five-year car loan is sixty (60) installment payments, when paid monthly.

Similarly, a thirty-year mortgage is 360 monthly installment payments. Both, revolving and installment debts have an interest rate attached to them that works against you. For instance, when using an auto loan calculator, a $20,000 loan financed for 60 months at a 5% interest rate would make your payment $377 a month, for a total repayment of $22,645. This means you will have paid $2,645 in interest at the end of the loan period. However, the same loan financed for 60 months at 10% interest rate would make your payment $425 per month for a total repayment of $25,496. Do you see the importance of obtaining the lowest interest rate when you have this type of debt? In the previous examples, the money that you owed did not double because the principal balance kept changing and going down each month you made a payment. Nevertheless, you still ended up paying more than you borrowed. That's our U.S. economy in a nutshell. Companies, banks, and businesses make money off of the debt that you owe.

Now ask yourself how many loans you have outstanding? Do they have interest rates attached to them? Let me list a few possible accounts you have:

1. Car note
2. Student Loan
3. Home Mortgage
4. Personal Loans
5. Credit Cards (How many?)
6. Store accounts

Now, make no mistake, I am not naïve. I know you need some credit in this world we live in. The problem is when you are charging everything you do in your daily life and never have cash to pay for your daily needs. When that happens, it is a great sign that you are living beyond your means and you are over-paying for everything with that interest rate working against you. Proverbs 22:7 NIV says, *"The rich rule over the poor, and the borrower is slave to the lender."* So, when possible, it is more beneficial to choose not to be poor nor get comfortable being a borrower.

After looking at how little most of us were taught about personal finances, you can see how a person can graduate college, work thirty years, and not have any money saved in their bank account when they retire. Once again, if you don't have a **vision** for your life and know your **purpose**, you can spend a whole lifetime making other people rich and not yourself or your family.

NOTES

- CHAPTER 3 -

CREDIT VS NET WORTH

In our world, we have two different economies that are promoted: credit score system and net worth system. When the business world refers to billionaires and millionaires, we tend to know them by name, due to our familiarity with their wealth's net worth. On the other hand, when the banking industry or business world speaks of the poor, or the working middle class, they tend to ask about their credit score. After all, a person's credit score determines the interest rate they will get when they borrow for a house, a car, or apply for a credit card. Similarly, the credit score you have may be used to determine if you get a particular job. Just like when background checks are required, they are used to help creditors make a judgement to rent an apartment or house to you or not. So, the creditors listed on your credit reports are extremely important and you should check them annually to make sure there isn't any identity theft issues attached to your name and social security number. Keep in mind, there are three credit bureaus to check and each will give you a free credit report, once a year.

Once you obtain a copy of your three credit reports, one from each credit bureau, review them thoroughly. If you find that you owe any old debts, once your budget permits, pay them off one at a time. My goal is to change your perspective going forward. I want you to start thinking in terms of net worth concerning your money, your life and your family's future.

The only way to start handing down generational wealth to your kids and grandkids is to unlearn how the world trained your mind to think about credit and net worth. Remember, the banks and different businesses are happy if you have to borrow your whole life for every day needs, like a set of tires for your car, furniture, appliances, or even the clothes you wear. They make money off of your borrowing. I want you to keep, save and invest your money because the way I see it, since you were the one who had to get up every day to go to work, you should get to keep some of the money for you and your family.

Hopefully, the Rule of 72 helps you choose a path most beneficial to you.

There are two versions of a bible verse that speaks volume to every ear that hears it regarding knowledge and choices:

> *The wise store up choice food and olive oils but*
> *fools gulp theirs down.*
> *Proverbs 21:20 NIV*

> *Wise people live in wealth and luxury, but stupid*
> *people spend their money as fast as they get it.*
> *Proverbs 21:20 GNT*

According to scripture, we must have a **plan** and use **wisdom** in breaking the cycle of living check to check, while being mindful of our credit reports and scores.

Choose today to start making **decisions** based on your net worth, so you can start to make better long-term **decisions** concerning your money and your life.

Long-Term Decisions vs. Short-Term Decisions

How many of you would like to work for a company that only makes short term **decisions**? Meaning, they are working hard on Tuesday just to make payroll on Friday. Or, would you be more at peace with a company that thinks long term, like thirty years out? They have a **plan** knowing their **purpose** and they are not worried about meeting payroll in the next two weeks. If you would prefer working for the long-term, **decision**-making company, then why wouldn't you want the same thing for you and your family's finances?

Let me make it plain. Let's say you are 90 years old and you have a perfect credit score of 850, three credit cards, a leased car that you still owe money on, and you live your whole life with payments. When you pass away, your children and grandchildren will not inherit your credit cards or excellent credit score. They won't even get to keep the leased car that was in your name. You would have lived a life having never applied the **discipline** to save cash because you got everything you wanted or needed with a signature. Is this the type of financial legacy you want to leave your family?

Now, let's look at the 90-year-old again, but under a different set of life principles. Let's say instead of spending a lifetime building your credit score, you built up your net worth, had cash in the bank and no credit cards. Instead of the leased car, your car was paid in full. So, when you passed away at 91 years old, things were different for your loved ones. In this instance, you used

wisdom and paid cash for things to be able to leave your children or grandchildren $130,000 cash in the bank, not including investments. You also left your family a car.

This is what generational wealth looks like when being handed down to the next generation.

"A good man leaves an inheritance to his children's children."

Proverbs 13:22 Part A ESV

Some people may think you can't save $130,000 in your local savings account. So, let's do the math and see if it's possible to do this. If the 90-year-old worked from age 22 years old to 65 years old, that is 43 years of employment. $130,000 divided by 43 years equals $3,023 a year. $3,023 a year divided by 12 months' equals $251.91 a month. Now you tell me, can you save $251.91 per month?

For those who say no, let me ask you this how much is your car note per month? How much is your credit card bill a month? How much is your cable bill a month? How much is your cell phone bill a month? How much do you spend on lunch at work per month? How much do you spend going out to eat on the weekends per month?

Once you add up the amounts spent on fast food and entertainment, I'm sure you could come up with $251 in a single-income household, or $126 per person in a two-income household to save each month.

I'm just trying to challenge you to think a different way and look at things from a few perspectives. You will often find out that you have the money, but you're just sending it out the door, instead of applying **discipline** or having a **vision**. Thinking long-term, knowing your **purpose**, and saving money are the best examples to model for you and your family.

In most cases, dealing with money, we don't have a lack of money problem or a lack of knowing basic math. Nobody wakes up on January 1 and says out loud, "I make $45,000 a year, but this year I'm going to spend $65,000." What we do have is a lack of **vision, planning**, and a lack of **discipline.**

So, the problem is that we get taken advantage of by the world's system. Although we don't say it out loud, we say it with our actions of overspending, borrowing, and charging. Then, at the end of the calendar year, we have truly spent $65,000, even though we only made $45,000. But really, it's more than that because we activated the Rule of 72 on all that borrowed money.

So, I strongly encourage parents to teach their children about net worth and talk to them about money, **planning, discipline** and patience concerning money. This is an invaluable life lesson that for all those that understand it and practice it will turn into valuable dollars later.

NOTES

- CHAPTER 4 -

WHAT ARE YOUR DREAMS AND PASSIONS?

Have you ever noticed that when that alarm clock rings at 6:00 a.m. to get up for work, some days your energy level is just not there? You get up anyway because that's called being a responsible adult and that job pays for your family's lifestyle and basic needs. On the other hand, if you're a person that likes to travel and you're taking a vacation to your favorite place, have you ever noticed when the same clock rings at 6:00 a.m. to wake you up for your flight, you're already awake before and full of energy ready to start your day. What's the difference? It's the same clock, the same 6:00 a.m., and the same person waking up in the same bed. The difference is the level of passion and excitement.

When the human mind and body is enthused, there is no limit to what you can accomplish. That's why to get the most out of your time, talent, life and money, you truly need to identify your dreams and passions. It's the thing that burns deep inside of your heart and your mind that you can't seem to forget about. It's always there to remind you. That's because, more than likely, it's tied to your **purpose.**

I believe everyone has a **purpose** and most people have more than one. For example, a little 7-year-old girl loves playing with her dolls and she's always telling her mom she's going to be a doctor when she grows up. Now at age 7, she has no idea about the cost of college, let alone the cost of Medical School. She doesn't know anything about having to pass certain tests like the MCAT and doesn't have a clue about malpractice insurance or working what see seems like 1000 hours a week during her residency. None of that changes the fact that at 7 years old, in her heart and mind, that little girl knew she had to be a doctor.

Acknowledging the dream and passion is always the first step of the journey. Then you jump over all the obstacles in life to accomplish that dream. You don't quit because it gets hard but persevere through the tough times considering the big picture, which is also the **vision.** That dream is worth all the sacrifices that you have to make to achieve the **goal**.

Now let's say the same 7-year-old girl is now 30 and a successful doctor. She also had dreams and **visions** of one day being married and having two children of her own. By 35, she was married and had two children. Her dreams and passions were really starting to unfold in her life as two of her main **goals** came to pass as she dreamed. Every person's dreams, **visions**, and **purpose** are different because the world needs different things from different people to complete the pieces of the puzzle called the human race. All pieces fit together to fulfill the big picture. Your time and money are two major parts in life that help you live out your dreams, **vision**s, and **purpose**. That is why we value these two resources so much.

NOTES

- CHAPTER 5 -

BUDGET AND EMERGENCY FUND

Why is it that we seem to look at people in a negative light when they ask us if we have a budget or are we living on one? A budget is when you write down your financial **plans** on paper for short-term and long-term **goals**.

So, if you know you like cold milk and orange juice out of your refrigerator, you have to pay the $100 light bill every month. Likewise, if you like watching your favorite television shows on cable, you have to pay the $130 cable bill each month. After that, if you like having extra money in your bank account, you must have **discipline** to save $100 or more every month that equals $1,200 a year saved, at least. Trust me, I'm not trying to tell you how to spend your money. I just want to get you to focus on your **goals**, wants and needs out of life. To start, ask yourself this question, "Do your money habits match what you say you want to accomplish out of your life?"

The point I'm trying to make is, in most cases, we earn enough money, but a lack of **discipline** and **planning** allows the money to get away from us. By the time we open our financial eyes, we notice that we made a lot of different industries around us wealthy, and we are not. Just as much as you are the one getting out of bed to go to work every day, you deserve to keep some of your cash earnings for all the hard work you do? Again, I'm not against the idea of purchasing newer cars or buying the best things for yourself. I'm just suggesting that you pay cash for the things you want out of life.

Now, if you find that you can't pay cash for the car you want, then **plan** on having a large down payment to make the monthly payment more manageable. Similar to a payment of $150 a month for 24 months. This is how you can use **discipline, wisdom,** and **planning** for your next big-ticket purchase. As a result, when you save extra money, in excess of your emergency fund, your dreams and passions can become a reality.

It is not realistic to believe that in January your goal is to have $1,200 saved by December and every time you get paid you spend $100 on pizza, going to the movies and shopping. I'm not against any of those things. I even love to do those same things from time to time, but neither of us should be missing out on our big picture **goals,** also known as **vision.** Let's not miss out on our **purpose** over pizza, movies or shopping. We can learn to do all those things with proper **planning** and budgeting, while using **wisdom** and **discipline.**

At the start of this chapter, I mentioned short-term and long-term **goals.** I would describe short-term **goals** as things that you want to accomplish in five years or less and long-term **goals** taking six years or more. However, before **planning** that out, start with the basics of your life: mortgage, rent, food, utilities, insurance payments (home owners, renter's insurance, car insurance, and life insurance), and gas money for the car, clothing, cell phone bill, charitable giving and an emergency fund.

Just to be clear, emergency funds are funds set aside for use when **unplanned** events happen, such as a loss of income. In life, we will encounter unexpected things.

Often, those things have a cost that we did not anticipate paying and this is where you need an emergency fund to help deal with it. It is designed to keep you from falling behind in your **planned** living expenses when the unexpected occurs.

Most financial experts say that an emergency fund should be three to six months of a person's living expenses. For example, if it takes $1,500 to run your household for one month, your emergency fund should be $4,500 to $9,000.

With this amount of cash saved, if you were to lose your job, you could run your household and meet all your financial obligations for three to six months off that savings. Earlier, when I listed some living expenses to run a household, I didn't list car notes, credit card bills, student loan debt, or individual store cards, since those are consumer debts.

Unlike living expenses, consumer debts are expenses that you can choose to pay off and not have them as bills anymore. Whereas, living expenses are things that typically do not have an end date and are ongoing, like utility bills. Even millionaires still have to pay utility bills.

Some people may think it's impossible to save up three to six months of expenses for an emergency fund, but it can be done. Many people have a car note that is $350 a month or more. Well, $350 multiplied by 12 months' equals $4,200 a year and $4,200 multiplied by five years equals $21,000 and I didn't even factor in the interest they paid on the loan. They just gave their emergency fund away to the auto industry and the bank that financed it. Likewise, many people may have had a car for five years with only a couple of payments left on it but decided to trade it in for a newer model for another five years of financing. Now when this happens, they end up paying

$350 a month for ten years, which equals $42,000 for financing those two cars.

When they look back over the past 10 years, they come to realize they spent over $42,000 in car payments, including interest. Yet, you keep telling yourself it is impossible to save $18,000 in your emergency fund. Well, that's not true. You just need to choose to pass your wealth to saving for an emergency, rather than the bank and auto industry.

Now let's look at credit card bills. As you may know, many people have credit cards and pay only the minimum due. For our example, if you had a credit card for five years and the minimum due was $200 a month, you would have paid that credit card company $12,000 cash, not including interest. Inasmuch as you were able to pay that amount to that credit card company, you could have saved that amount towards your emergency fund. This proves that you are capable, but you just need to redirect your **discipline** to invest in yourself. Don't you think you and your family deserve that $12,000 more than the credit card company?

An emergency fund is needed, no matter what part of the country you live in. Different things can happen that affect you and your family: floods, fires, tornados, hurricanes, and forest fires. Life is always happening and changing quickly and not always for the better. It is full of new challenges, but you don't have to deal with those problems being stressed and without money. For instance, let's look at two similar scenarios. In the first one, there is a family that experienced a house fire and lost everything but got out safely. Typically, you see this on your local news as reporters are requesting donations for the family, while they are staying at a local shelter.

Unfortunately, that family did not have homeowner's or renter's insurance. I pray your family never goes through any tragic loss caused by these harsh, unfair circumstances that life may send your way. In the second scenario, a family lost everything due to a fire and all family members got out safely. This time, the local news reported that the family had an emergency fund and were able to stay in a nice hotel. They had full coverage insurance and will be expecting a check from the insurance company to cover their loss. After seeing those two scenarios, which story would you prefer for your family? Hopefully, you would choose the latter and agree with me that your family needs an emergency fund.

Overall, both budgeting and emergency funds play a huge part in our lives and it is up to us to determine how much.

NOTES

- Chapter 6 -

Consumer Debt

The economy we live in promotes consumer debt, so many of us have accepted it as a normal way of life. Our government and most businesses earn their profits off the money that we borrow that has an interest rate attached to it. For example, you go to your local bank and open a savings or checking account and they tell you your account will earn .05% on money deposited. Then, 30 days later, you get a credit card in the mail from that same bank that is pre-approved at 11.99%. If you accept and use it, but don't pay off the balance in full each month, the bank wins that money deal. Remember the Rule of 72.

In order to have a good **plan**, you should be able to list all your consumer debts on paper and know the exact date each one will be paid off. The **goal** for you is to live with **vision**, **purpose** and **wisdom** to guide your everyday **decisions**. Remember this, *"The rich rule over the poor, and the borrower is slave to the lender"* Proverbs 22:7 NIV

So let's say you have 10 different consumer debt accounts, like the average married couple below:

    1 Home Mortgage at $250,000
    2 car notes at $13,000 and $18,000
    3 credit cards at $6,000, $4,000, and $3,500

2 student loans at $37,000 and $22,000
1 store charge card at $1,700
1 personal loan at $2,400

In this example, the married couple has 10 different "masters" who they have to give an account to and send money to each month. By masters, I mean the ten consumer accounts that make this couple work hard to repay them.

It's only when this couple decides that they are tired of being slaves to these 10 different masters that they use **wisdom** and pay off the smallest bill together, which is $1,700. Since they both work and get paid every two weeks, that's four pays a month between the two of them. They can start sending four payments a month to the store card to get it down to zero and commit to not use it again. Meanwhile, they continue to send minimum payments to the other nine creditors. Once the $1,700 account is at zero, the next bill they pay down together is the $2,400 personal loan. This is where their **discipline** and patience will be tested, as they keep the rhythm making these payments until all accounts are paid in full. Remember, they didn't get into debt in one day and there are not going to get out of debt in one day.

Before reading this book, you might have had several years of bad financial habits and no **plan** to correct them. So, now, the main thing is to get your mindset changed and allow yourself to see things through a different perspective as you start to act right with your money and let it do its job.

After reading this book, you will no longer be a helpless financial victim that can't get ahead financially. You will be victorious in finance, as you choose daily not to be defeated in this area of life.

*"A good man leaves and inheritance to his
children's children."*

Proverbs 13:22 Part A ESV

Decide to leave an inheritance for your immediate family,
your local church, college alma mater or a local charity in
your community. Leave your assets for them to benefit
from, upon your passing, rather than bills. All our time,
talent, and treasures should help make this world a better
place and contribute to our families having a better life.

NOTES

- CHAPTER 7 -

INVESTMENTS

According to Webster's dictionary, an investment is defined as an act of devoting time, effort, or energy to a particular undertaking with the expectation of a worthwhile result. Once those concepts are clear, you can better understand that investments involve you managing your money and making decisions that helps you and your family accomplish all the **goals** you have set.

For instance, a short-term goal would be realizing you have a 13-year-old son that is going to need his own car in the next three years, since he's going to be really active by age 16 with football, track practice, and a part-time job. So, as a parent, you decide you are willing to save $3,000 for his car. That means you have 36 months to save the $3,000 you decided to pay for a decent, used car. When you break it down, it is $3,000 divided by 36 months, which equals $83.33 per month. This a good example of a short-term goal, due to its timeframe of three years.

On the other hand, an example of a long-term goal, which is six years or more, could be illustrated by a woman that wants her kitchen remodeled. She wants hardwood floors, new cabinets and stainless-steel appliances professionally installed. The total cost is $40,000 and she

plans to pay it off in eight years. Now that we know the amount of the remodel and the number of years to pay it off, we can determine the monthly amount to save by dividing $40,000 by 96 months, which equals $416.66 a month. So, in this example she would agree to save $416.66, per month, for eight years to reach her goal of saving $40,000 for this project. This task requires a lot of patience as most people won't wait eight years to save for something they really want now. More often, some people would borrow the $40,000 and finance it for eight years at 9% interest. Their monthly payment would be $586 a month and the total cost for this financed project would be $56,256.78! Either way, a person would have to make a conscious decision to save for the remodel and pay $40,000 cash or finance the remodel and pay over $56,000 to have it right now. It really comes down to what are you are willing to do, since you would be the one getting up every day going to work for it.

Another long-term investment example would be a college fund. This works best when you start saving when your child is one-year-old, and you have 17 years to fund a 529 **plan**, which is designed to be a tax advantage for a designated beneficiary for college. Similarly, you may decide to start an UGMA (Uniform Gift to Minors Act) or UTMA (Uniform Transfers to Minors Act) account. Each family needs to do their own research to decide which **plan** is best for their child and household budget.

Be sure you make provisions to invest in your own retirement. There will come a time when you are going to be 65 years old and be retiring, voluntarily or involuntarily, from your job. Either way, you will need to be proactive and have a **plan**, so you will not have to scramble for solutions in your golden years. If your employer has a 401(k) or 403(b) **plan**, please join and make sure you invest enough to get the employer match, if one is offered. Once your consumer debts are paid off, ask your human resource representative what the maximum percentage is you can pay into those plans.

However, "don't put all your eggs in one basket". I encourage you to use **wisdom** and open a ROTH IRA, which is an individual retirement account that is separate from your employer's 401(k). This way, you have two retirement vehicles that are both doing well and growing at nice interest rates, annually. Most expert financial advisors suggest that you save between ten to twenty percent of your annual income for your retirement. Of course, the earlier you start the better. Remember the Rule of 72.

You may have also invested in some stocks or mutual funds. These, unlike the ROTH IRA, may not necessarily be tied to a retirement account but just something that you invested in. You may see these in everyday products that you are using or have in your home. Just think of the brand of washing powder you use or maker of the car you drive as a stock option. Whereas, a mutual fund is like a big umbrella that may have multiple companies under its name that are still tied to the stock market. Nevertheless, individual stocks are riskier than mutual funds.

Investments like these can have the Rule of 72 working positively for you. So, **plan** to talk with a Financial Advisor to gain clarity for all the risk involved. It's okay to shop around as you do your research before investing because some investments may have fees depending on what type you are trying to acquire.

Be sure to continue to read and gain knowledge about your finances. Ask questions, because this is your life, your time, your money. Don't depend totally on another person to love you and have your best interest concerning your money and your family's livelihood more than you.

> Get **wisdom**, get understanding; do not forget my
> words or turn away from them. Do not forsake
> **wisdom**, and she will protect you; love her, and
> she will watch over you. The beginning of **wisdom**
> is this: Get **wisdom**. Though it cost you all you
> have, get understanding.
>
> Proverbs 4:5-7 NIV

NOTES

- CHAPTER 8 -

SHORT-TERM VS. LONG-TERM THINKING

How many people wake up January 1 knowing that they make $50,000 a year and say, "This year, I'm going to spend $70,000 without making any provisions to get a second job or some extra income"? As crazy as that sounds, many people do it all the time. Our lack of **planning** and ability to make short-term **decisions** result in bad choices as we overspend. How a person handles and spends their money has much to do with their mindset and little to do with math or money.

Some of us recklessly charge on credit cards, borrow cash, apply for a second mortgage, sign up with pay day loan lenders or a car title loan places and then complain, by December, that we are broke. These are financial habits that indicate a short-term thinking mindset. Each of them shows a lack of **discipline** and giving in to untimely impulses. After all that, some of us have the nerve to wonder how we overspent by $20,000.

Historically, most successful people think long-term, which means they make daily **decisions** considering how it will affect them years from now. They also tend to stay away from quick impulsions that will negatively impact their future. In the spur of the moment, many **decisions** may seem good, but in the long run may be bad for you and your family's long-term future.

I'm not saying it is easy to change your financial situation overnight, but I am saying it is worth it. When you do, you are literally changing the cycle of you and your family's life for the better. Your new mindset gives your family a better chance later, and more opportunities to change the situation.

If you don't have a high-paying job to help change your situation, then find a like-minded family member and agree to share an apartment and split the bills. This way, you both can save and work the temporary **plan** you both have decided upon, while holding each other accountable to your individual **visions** and **plans**. Remember there is strength in numbers!

I'm not saying do this forever, but the two of you should sit down to set a timeframe of about one to three years that could be beneficial for both of you. This would be far better than each of you struggling for the next few years separately. Likewise, if you don't have a family member, the same could be done with a best friend or college roommate that can hold you accountable to the **vision** and the **plan.** The key to this is to partner with a trusted, responsible individual.

For me, one of the things I did at 18 was join the Air Force. I figured if I get free meals and free rent that would give me the ability to save money and change my life's trajectory, as I proudly served my country for four years. The bonus was that I also got to travel and see the world.

For others, it may be just getting a second job for a period of time to help pay down bills and build their emergency fund. The main ingredient is a **vision** for your life and then having a practical **plan** to reach all of your **goals.**

Once you dig out of your financial hole and build up your savings, now you are becoming a long-term thinker. You are now better equipped to handle purchasing big ticket items, now that you know the difference between sticker price and the cost of financing. You get to exercise your **discipline** and avoid that Rule of 72 working against you.

Here are a few examples to further explain financed purchases:

Example 1: You buy a one-year old car from the dealership at $25,000 on a five-year loan. The sticker says $25,000, but with financing at 5% interest, you really pay $28,306.

Example 2: You buy a $200,000 house on a 30-year mortgage. The selling price is $200,000, but the 30-year mortgage at 4.52% interest with $20,000 down payment really means you will be paying 360 monthly payments of $914.17. The total principle on this house is now $180,000 and the total interest will be $149,102.58. So, by the time this mortgage is paid off, that $200,000 house ends up costing you over $349,000! Once again, I want you to be well-informed and aware when you are signing up for a loan, so that you know exactly what it will cost you every time.

"Suppose one of you wants to build a tower. Won't you first sit down and estimate the cost to see if you have enough money to complete it?"
Luke 14:28 (NIV)

You were not created to live your whole life under stress and financial problems. Hardships cause a lot of stress. Any doctor will tell you that stress causes many side effects to the body: anxiety, insomnia, headaches, ulcers, migraines, weight loss, weight gain, or hair breakage, in some cases, due to stress. In some extreme cases, stress can cause high blood pressure, stroke, or even heart attack. So, why would you ever want to live your whole adult life under a cloud of financial stress? We, as humans, should never worship money, but make wise **decisions** concerning it, since it affects every area of our lives.

For example, if I gave you $2 million dollars but you were $10 million dollars in debt, you would still have stress on you wondering how you could come up with the other $8 million that you owe. On the other hand, if I gave you $200,000 and you were already debt-free, you would feel so happy. Often, it's not the amount of money, but **contentment** and a stress-free environment that leads to having joy and peace.

NOTES

- CHAPTER 9 -

WILL YOU BE A VICTIM OR VICTORIOUS?

Hopefully you have noticed a pattern through the first eight chapters. Having a **plan**, a **vision**, knowing your **purpose**, obtaining knowledge, having patience, applying **discipline** and **wisdom**, when thinking long-term, all help you to make better financial **decisions**.

You may not have received a big pay raise, but when applying these principles and attributes to this area of your life, it seems like your money accomplishes more. Well, this is the time you have to **decide** for yourself if you are going to be a victim that always has money problems, lives check to check, and always has to borrow from people or pay day loan lenders; or if you are going to live victorious in this area of your life.

Remember, in most cases, it's not the lack of money that causes money problems, but a lack of **discipline**. The wrong mindset about money leads to many money problems.

A true lack of money typically results from things like job loss, divorce, and death of a spouse in a two-income family, serious health issues and long hospital stays. At these points and times in life, it's hard and seems unfair what has happened to you. I still don't want you to fall into the victim mindset. Take some time to grieve the loss you have experienced because you need that time to heal the emotional pain you are going through. Nevertheless, I want you to maintain a victorious mindset that you will devise a **plan** to overcome this huge setback. Make choices to make changes for the better. However, maybe you don't have the strength or know how to get back on track. If so, acknowledge that and find someone who's been through the same thing or join a support group to talk through all those life issues. Remember, there is a great **purpose** for your life that dwells on the inside and the world is waiting on you to bring it forth and deposit it into society.

So, I truly encourage you to choose the victorious mindset regarding your finances and all other areas in your life.

NOTES

- CHAPTER 10 -

DREAM BOARD/VISION BOARD

What is the dream or **vision** that you keep thinking about in your sub-conscience that you just can't get out of your head or heart? If money was no object, what would you be doing with your time in this life? What is your natural passion? Now, I want you to make a dream board. Buy yourself a large piece of construction paper about 13" x 24" or larger. Then find old magazines around the house and cut out pictures and tape or glue them to your dream board of the things you want to accomplish. You can also mix in some family pictures and inspirational sayings on your dream board.

Some examples could be the following: graduate from college, buy a house, pay off debt, getting married, have a baby, put the kids through school, buy a certain type of car, find a job, find a dream job, move out of town, help volunteer at your local charity, fix up an old house, adopt kids, become a foster parent, start a business, travel, retire from your job, take a cruise, learn to surf, climb a mountain, skydive etc. It could be whatever you feel that you are working for that helps you fulfill your **purpose** to help make your life complete.

Since everyone has a different **purpose**, each person's dream board will look different. As you list with words and collect pictures of all the things you want to accomplish in your future, write dates by each one of them to hold yourself accountable to attaining those **goals**. Make sure you don't keep saying, "One of these days I'm going to do this or that." As you accomplish each one, put a checkmark next to it, so you can see the progress you are making and teach your kids, family and friends how to make their own dream boards. This will ensure that all the people in your circle will become better long-term thinkers and **planners**.

Accomplishing your dreams or **vision**s may take a while to check off. It could take from six months to five years or more. The point is that the pictures on your board help you make better daily **decisions** to fulfill the **goals** you have **planned**.

Once complete, hang your dream board up somewhere in your house or apartment, so that you can see it on a regular basis as a reminder of what you said you wanted to do with your life. Then, find yourself an accountability partner. This will be someone you share your dreams and **visions** with who has your permission to speak into your life. They will ask you from time to time what **decisions** have you made towards making sure your future dreams and **goals** come true.

In conclusion, I hope something in this book has been of some help to you as you move forward in your financial life and be a blessing for generations to come in your family.

Your humble servant,
Brian Stephens

NOTES

TOOLS FOR YOUR JOURNEY

If you are paid bi-weekly, this means there are two months in a year when you will receive three pays in a month. It's important to have a plan for the months that you will receive a 3rd pay check, whether it's saving it, or paying down debt.

1st Pay	2nd Pay	3rd Pay
Gross	Gross	Gross
Net	Net	Net
Tithes	Tithes	Tithes
Savings	Savings	Savings
Pocket Money	Pocket Money	Pocket Money
Bill	Bill	Bill
Bill	Bill	Bill
Bill	Bill	Bill
Bill	Bill	Bill
Bill	Bill	Bill
Bill	Bill	Bill
Bill	Bill	Bill
Bill	Bill	Bill
Bill	Bill	Bill
Bill	Bill	Bill
Bill	Bill	Bill
Bill	Bill	Bill
Bill	Bill	Bill
Bill	Bill	Bill

Consumer Debt Reduction Sheet

List the amount of your bills from Smallest to Largest.

Then, focus on paying as much as you can on the smallest bill, while paying the minimum on all the rest.

Bill Name	Bill Balance	Bill Interest Rate	Bill Due Date	Amount Paid - Min	Amount Paid - Extra	Expected Pay Off Date

Use this chart to help you build your emergency fund, and once that's done. Use this same chart to build up your everyday saving account.

Remember, this is not an investment account, but a saving account to give your family a peace of mind.

	3 Yrs.	5 Yrs.	7 Yrs.	10 Yrs.	15 Yrs.
100 Month	$3600	$6000	$8400	$12000	$18000
200 Month	$7200	$12000	$16800	$24000	$36000
300 Month	$10800	$18000	$25200	$36000	$54000
400 Month	$14400	$24000	$33600	$48000	$72000
500 Month	$18000	$30000	$42000	$60000	$90000

*0% Interest Just Cash Savings

HOW LONG IT TAKES YOUR MONEY TO DOUBLE: RULE OF 72

72/1% = 72 Years	72/15% = 4 Years and 8 Months
72/3% = 24 Years	72/18% = 4 Years
72/6% = 12 Years	72/21% = 3 Years and 4 Months
72/10% = 7 Years and 2 Months	72/24% = 3 Years
72/12% = 6 Years	72/29% = 2 Years and 4 Months

Here are a few examples for my married couples to help keep financial tension out of the relationship, and to keep working together as a team.

Let's look at example 1: Your wife wants a designer handbag that cost $1,000.00. For a two income household, the couple will commit to saving $100.00 per pay.

This will equal one thousand dollars in two and a half months. Now, the wife can purchase from her wish list and pay cash.

Let's look at example 2: Your husband has a $1,000.00 balance on his credit card he want to pay off. So now the wife will help him, both committing to paying $100.00 a pay check to get rid of the debt in two and half months.

This is what you call a **WIN-WIN**!

Just remember couples to keep the wish list dollar amounts about even and it should work out just fine. The wish list doesn't have to consist of buying something new

Wish List

1. HERS

2. HIS

3. HERS

4. HIS

5. HERS

6. HIS

7. HERS

8. HIS

9. HERS

10. HIS

Bonus Tip

If a financial advisor advises you to not pay your home off early because you will lose your ability to write it off on your taxes, don't listen to them.

If you make $100,000 a year and your monthly mortgage payment is $1,000.00 per month that equals $12,000 a year. Out of the $12,000 you paid, $4000 of it is paid to the bank as interest. As a result, you get to claim that $4,000 in interest payments as a tax write off. Since most people are in the 24% tax bracket, 24% of $4,000 is $960. This means you gave the bank $12,000 to get a tax savings of $960.

On the other hand, you could pay your home off early and donate $4,000 to your local church, charity, non-profit organization or college. By doing it this way, you would receive the same $960 tax savings and keep the $8,000 you once gave the bank for mortgage payments in your bank account. So, choose to be wise and pay your home off early. You will not regret it

ABOUT THE AUTHOR

Brian Stephens is a proud U.S. Air Force Veteran, who is currently working in the Utilities Industry for over 19 years.

He teaches a finance class as part of the Christian Education Team at New Community Bible Fellowship in Cleveland Heights, Ohio.

Brian has a passion for helping people in the area of finance. He shows them how to follow their dreams and be free from the pressures of financial stress.

Contact Information

You can reach Brian on Twitter @7Prosperous to share your new found victories over this constant challenge of finance.